United Nations

Linda Melvern

W
FRANKLIN WATTS
A Division of Scholastic Inc.
NEW YORK TORONTO LONDON AUCKLAND SYDNEY
MEXICO CITY NEW DELHI HONG KONG
DANBURY, CONNECTICUT

AP

Picture credits:
Cover: Panos: left (Howard Davies), right above (Giacomo Pirozzi); United Nations: right below. Inside: Corbis: 3 (Reuters/Chris Helgren), 22b (Reuters/Chris Helgren). Magnum Photos: 1, 7 (David Seymour), 9 (Sergio Larrain), 14t (Abbas), 14b (Luc Delahaye), 15 (Bruno Barbey), 20, 21 (Paul Lowe), 22t (Bruno Barbey), 25b (David Seymour). Panos Pictures: 5l (Crispin Hughes), 8r (Howard Davies), 18 (Crispin Hughes), 19 (Paul Smith), 23 (Betty Press), 25t (Giacomo Pirozzi), 27t (Jean-Léo Dugast). Rex Features: 11t (Sipa), 11b, 12t (Sipa), 12b (Sipa). Still Pictures: 11 (Teit Hornbak), 2t (Mark Edwards), 2–3 (Gary Trotter), 5r (Teit Hornbak), 10 (Harmut Schwarzbach), 26 (Mark Edwards), 28r (Jorgen Schytte), 28l (Mark Edwards), 29 (Gary Trotter). Topham Picturepoint: 6, 17t, 17b (Associated Press), 24, 27b. United Nations: 3br, 4, 8l (UN photo 185265/A. Brizzi), 13 (UN photo 179194/Milton Grant), 16l (UN photo 18266/Fabrice Ribere), 16r (UN/DPI/Milton Grant)

First published in 2001 by Franklin Watts

Series Editor: Anderley Moore
Designer: Simon Borrough
Picture Research: Sue Mennell
Consultant: Ahmad Fawzi, Director, United Nations Information Centre, London

First American edition 2001 by Franklin Watts
A Division of Grolier Publishing
90 Sherman Turnpike
Danbury, CT 06816

Visit Franklin Watts on the Internet at:
http://publishing.grolier.com

Catalog-in-Publication Data is available from the Library of Congress
ISBN   0-531-14624-3 (lib. bdg.)
ISBN   0-531-14814-9 (pbk.)

1. What Is the United Nations?

The United Nations was created at the end of World War II (1939–45). When this terrible war was over, people everywhere were longing for a better world.

▼ *The creation of the UN in 1945 was marked by a special ceremony in San Francisco to sign the charter. Here, the British ambassador signs the charter.*

● Spotlight

"We the peoples of the United Nations are determined to save succeeding generations from the scourge of war, which twice in our lifetime has brought untold sorrow to mankind."

—The UN Charter, 1945

▲ *The official emblem of the UN shows a world map bordered by branches from an olive tree — a symbol of peace.*

A Dream of Peace

On October 24, 1945, fifty-one of the world's governments joined together to form the United Nations. They agreed to work together to try to make the world a more peaceful and prosperous place. There are now 189 countries that are members of the UN and that are committed to achieving its aims.

Goals and Responsibilities

The goals of the UN are listed in the UN Charter. The charter also states how these goals should be carried out and outlines the responsibilities of UN members, their rights, and their duties. In the charter, the governments pledge to live together in peace as good neighbors.

▲ The UN helps those suffering as a result of war. Here it provides food for people in war-torn Rwanda.

Working Together

The UN does not have any power over its member countries. It relies on its members to follow the goals and the principles in the charter and the decisions and guidelines adopted by the UN. Ultimately, it is up to each member government to decide if it wishes to cooperate.

▼ A UN peacekeeper helps people in Cambodia return home following civil war. They had been staying in refugee camps in Thailand for safety.

◐ Problem

Since the UN was created in 1945

- over 30 million people have been killed in war, most of them unarmed civilians
- over 100 million people have fled their homes because of conflict
- governments have invested more money in preparing for war than in strengthening peace

The Ideas Behind the UN

Ever since it was created, the UN has tried to set basic standards for the whole world to follow. In 1948, it created a document called the Universal Declaration of Human Rights. This outlined the rights that the UN believed everyone in the world has. These are your rights too.

▼ *This sculpture of a gun with a knot in the barrel symbolizes the UN's dedication to peace. It stands at the entrance to the UN Secretariat building in New York City.*

What Are Our Human Rights?

The Universal Declaration of Human Rights declares that people have the right to life, freedom, and security. It states that people should be free from slavery, they should have the right to a fair trial, the right to marry and to own property, and the right to believe in whatever religion they choose.

Denying Rights

Although the declaration was agreed on in 1948, many governments still fail to give their people their rights. The UN tries to monitor any country that is breaking these rules through a special organization called the UN Commission on Human Rights. By doing this, the UN makes sure that the rest of the world is aware of the country's human rights record. This makes it harder for the country to get away with human rights abuses.

▼ *Eleanor Roosevelt talks to a colleague during a break from a UN meeting in 1951.*

✓ Checklist

The Universal Declaration of Human Rights states that

- everyone has the right to freedom of movement
- everyone has the right to work
- everyone has the right to equal pay for equal work
- everyone has the right to rest and leisure
- everyone has the right to education

● Spotlight

Eleanor Roosevelt, wife of U.S. president Franklin D. Roosevelt, helped write the Universal Declaration of Human Rights. She decided to do this following a visit to Germany after World War II. While there, she had seen for herself the destruction of war. The drafting of this document was the result of two years' work. It took a long time for all the member countries to agree on what the declaration should say, but Eleanor Roosevelt was very persistent, and in 1948 the declaration was completed.

When Eleanor Roosevelt died in 1962, a U.S. statesman, Adlai Stevenson, said of her, "She would rather light candles than curse the darkness, and her glow has warmed the world."

2. How the UN Works

✅ Checklist

The UN is made up of
- the Secretariat
- the General Assembly
- the Security Council
- the Economic and Social Council
- the Trusteeship Council
- the International Court of Justice

◀ *An aerial view of the United Nations U.S. headquarters (known as the Secretariat) in New York City.*

The UN is divided into six parts. Each part has an important and different role to play in the UN system.

The Secretariat

There are people working for the UN in many parts of the world, and there are UN offices in most countries. The headquarters of the UN, known as the Secretariat, is in New York City. Over 8,700 staff members from all around the world work there. They include economists, translators, secretaries, computer experts, security guards, librarians, lawyers, writers, and journalists.

When someone works for the UN, he or she promises loyalty to the UN and may not seek or receive any orders from any government. The governments, in turn, promise not to influence the staff of the UN in any way.

▲ *The entrance to the UN offices in Geneva — one of the three main regional offices of the Secretariat. The other two are in Vienna and Nairobi.*

✅ Checklist

The UN has six official languages: Arabic, Russian, Spanish, English, French, and Chinese.

The General Assembly

The General Assembly is a big meeting at which every member country of the UN is represented. The General Assembly decides how the UN will spend its budget and makes decisions on world issues. To make a decision or pass a resolution, two-thirds of the member countries must vote in favor.

The General Debate

Once a year, all the members of the UN send representatives to the Secretariat for meetings to discuss any world crises and catastrophes. The main meeting is called the General Debate, and in this debate, all member countries can express their views on a wide range of issues. Most world leaders have addressed the General Debate of the General Assembly.

▲ Many world leaders have addressed the General Assembly in New York. Here, Cuban head of state Fidel Castro delivers a speech to UN member countries in 1960.

Problem

Each time the cost of the UN rises, the United States' share of this cost also increases. Some American politicians have argued that the UN is too expensive, and they question why the United States has to pay so much. Some have argued that the U.S. contribution should be reduced. Meanwhile, the debt the United States owes the UN increases all the time.

Who Pays for the UN?

The costs of the United Nations are shared by its members. Each one pays a different amount. The founders of the United Nations decided that the world's rich countries should pay more for the UN than the world's poor countries. The United States is the world's richest country, so it pays more than any other UN member. Many of the world's poorest countries, including Rwanda, Sierra Leone, Mauritania, Cambodia, St. Kitts, and Nevis, pay only a small amount toward the UN.

The Economic and Social Council

The UN's founders believed that reducing the amount of poverty in the world would help create world peace. The Economic and Social Council was set up to coordinate all UN efforts to improve the standards of living of the world's poor. The UN works to bring full employment and create conditions of economic and social progress and development. As much as 70 percent of the work of the UN system is devoted to accomplishing this task.

▼ *A UN food aid mission delivers food parcels by plane during the UN-assisted Food Aid Program to help famine victims in the Sudan in 1994.*

✔ Checklist

The eleven countries in the original Trusteeship Council were:
1. Togoland (under British administration)
2. Somaliland (under Italian administration)
3. Togoland (under French administration)
4. Cameroons (under French administration)
5. Cameroons (under British administration)
6. Tanganyika (under British administration)
7. Ruanda-Urundi (under Belgian administration)
8. Western Samoa (under New Zealand administration)
9. Nauru (under Australian administration)
10. New Guinea (under Australian administration)
11. Trust Territory of the Pacific Islands:
Federal States of Micronesia; Republic of the Marshall Islands; Commonwealth of the Northern Mariana Islands; Palau (under United States administration)

Trusteeship Council

The Trusteeship Council is not as important as it once was. It was created to look after eleven territories that had no government, and were therefore under international control. The trusteeship was charged with ensuring that governments responsible for the territories' administration helped them prepare to govern themselves. All these territories are now self-governing.

The International Court of Justice

The International Court of Justice at The Hague, the Netherlands, is the world's court. It hears cases in which one nation blames another for wrongdoing. For example, in 1949 the UK took Norway to the International Court over fishing rights. The court ruled that Norway was within its rights to reserve certain fishing grounds for its own boats. International law applies to all countries. The court is not open to individual people. It is only open to governments. The UN General Assembly and the Security Council can ask the court for an opinion on any legal question.

Problem

In 1971, the court ruled that South Africa, a member of the UN, must cease its occupation of the territory of Namibia and leave. South Africa did not abide by the court ruling, despite the UN Charter's call on each UN member to accept the decisions of this court.

◀ The International Court of Justice at The Hague, the Netherlands.

▼ Judges of the United Nations International Court of Justice.

Spotlight

In 1979 the U.S. Embassy was seized in Teheran, Iran. Staff members were taken hostage, and the U.S. government filed an application for their release at the United Nations International Court of Justice. The court found that Iran was violating international law and that the hostages must be released.

Checklist

The court has the right to rule on

- breaches in treaties and agreements between states
- questions of international law
- the interpretation of treaties
- the nature or extent of reparations to be made for breach of an international obligation

◄ U.S. Embassy employees are blindfolded and paraded before the world's press in Teheran, Iran.

▼ Iranian terrorists seize control of the U.S. Embassy building in Teheran, Iran, 1979.

The most powerful part of the UN is the Security Council — a meeting of representatives from fifteen countries in the UN. The Security Council has responsibility for the world's international peace and security. All member countries are bound by the UN Charter to obey the council.

▼ *The first ever meeting of the Security Council held at summit level took place in January 1992. The world's leaders promised to cooperate with the UN in their efforts to maintain world peace.*

Permanent Seats

Of the UN's 189 members, only fifteen are allowed to sit on the Security Council. Only five of those countries are permanent members of the council. These five are the countries who won World War II: China, the United States, the UK, France, and Russia. These five members have a veto in the council, which means that they can stop any decision they do not like.

Extra Seats

Ten other countries are represented on the Security Council. These sit in the ten nonpermanent positions, and they are chosen by the General Assembly. They sit in the council for two years, then ten different countries are chosen. The presidency of the Security Council also changes — it is held by a different country each month.

Preventing War

When there are disagreements between countries, first and foremost, it is the job of the Security Council to mediate between them — to try to help them sort out any arguments before they escalate into war.

If one country is being attacked by another country, it can turn to the UN for help. There are then several things that the Security Council can do. The Security Council can try to stop UN members from trading with the aggressive country. It can send negotiators to help the countries resolve their differences. The council can forbid countries to sell arms to aggressive countries. This is called an arms embargo.

Sometimes the Security Council gives the authority for countries to take military action. This was the case when Iraq invaded Kuwait in 1990. In this instance, the United States led a group of countries to force Iraq to withdraw from Kuwait. This military coalition was agreed to by the Security Council.

▲ British troops involved in the liberation of Kuwait from Iraqi invasion, 1990.

▼ UN peacekeepers from France are seen guarding the airport in Sarajevo, Bosnia, during the civil war that followed the collapse of Yugoslavia.

A World Police Force

When the UN was created, the council was to be the world police force, making sure all the countries abided by international laws. The founders of the UN believed that in order to have a stable world, the Security Council must have the means to prevent conflict — with force if necessary.

Some people have suggested that Germany and Japan should be allowed permanent seats because of their economic power. Large countries such as Brazil and India are seeking more power in the UN. Discussions about changes to the Security Council have been taking place for some years with no agreement. The permanent five seem unwilling to give up their power.

▲ *UN peacekeepers from Japan, wearing the distinctive blue beret of their uniform, disembark from their UN transport plane in Cambodia.*

Time for Reform?

The decision to have five permanent members on the Security Council was made when the UN was created in 1945. The world has changed a great deal since then, and the UN has grown. Some member countries argue that this should be reflected in the Security Council.

The UN is headed by one person — the secretary-general. He or she must ensure that the UN operates efficiently and that the whole UN family is working well together and coordinating its activities. The secretary-general has to try to please all UN members, particularly the five most powerful states — the permanent members of the Security Council.

✅ Checklist

The seven secretaries-general of the UN and their nationalities:
1. Trygve Lie, Norway, 1946–1952
2. Dag Hammarskjold, Sweden, 1953–1961
3. U Thant, Burma (now called Myanmar), 1961–1971
4. Kurt Waldheim, Austria, 1972–1981
5. Javier Perez de Cuellar, Peru, 1982–1991
6. Boutros Boutros-Ghali, Egypt, 1992–1996
7. Kofi Annan, Ghana, 1997–

▲ Boutros Boutros-Ghali visits a UN-supported orphanage in Somalia accompanied by a commander of UN peacekeepers.

▶ Unlike previous secretaries-general, Kofi Annan was chosen from the staff members of the UN Secretariat, where he had worked for 30 years.

The Role of the Secretary-General

In the eyes of the world, the secretary-general stands for the UN as a whole. The secretary-general is said to be a spokesperson for all humankind. The holder of this office must try to persuade the member countries to uphold the ideals outlined in the charter. This has been called the most impossible job in the world — although all UN members have signed the charter, all countries want to follow their own interests.

▲ *Kofi Annan meets Saddam Hussein in Baghdad in 1998 in an effort to persuade the Iraqi leader to allow UN weapons inspectors to assess the extent of Iraq's military strength.*

The secretary-general has to warn the Security Council about any problems that may threaten the peace and security of any member country. The secretary-general has a duty to act as a mediator when conflict threatens; when member countries are at loggerheads, the secretary-general must do all he or she can in order to avoid conflict.

◀ *Inspectors from the UN Special Commission, UNSCOM, in Baghdad. It was their job to ensure the elimination of Iraq's weapons of mass destruction.*

5. UN Peacekeepers

The main goal of the United Nations is to create a world free from war. Sometimes the only way to keep the peace is to have soldiers acting as a police force in a war zone to stop the fighting. The United Nations has soldiers for peace called peacekeepers.

What Is Peacekeeping?

Peacekeeping grew out of the need to have neutral soldiers standing between two enemies. After international politicians and UN negotiators have persuaded two enemies to come to an agreement, UN soldiers go into the area to make sure the enemies obey the cease-fires and truces that have been negotiated.

Peacekeepers rely on persuasion and minimal force to defuse tensions and prevent fighting. It is dangerous work.

Peacekeeping Today

UN peacekeepers also help countries recover from a war. Peacekeeping today is a combination of political, military, and humanitarian action. Police officers, election observers, human rights monitors, and other civilians (non-soldiers) go with soldiers into war zones as UN peacekeepers.

▼ UN peacekeepers from Italy prepare to destroy arms and tanks surrendered by warlords in Somalia.

Peacekeepers sometimes help get food to people who are starving and try to make sure people have water that is clean. Peacekeepers can provide stability so that the parties do not renew their violence and slide back into war. Sometimes UN peacekeepers watch elections to ensure they are held fairly.

▼ A UN peacekeeper from Italy gives candy to children orphaned in the Mozambique civil war.

✅ Checklist

- In Namibia, UN peacekeepers helped the people elect their own government and create a new and independent nation.
- In Mozambique, UN peacekeepers helped organize free and fair elections.
- In El Salvador, UN peacekeepers helped reform a corrupt government and monitor the end of ten years of civil war.
- In Guatemala, the UN helped establish a new human rights procedure to make sure people were no longer afraid because of violence and killing.

The Price of Peace

Since 1948, there have been fifty-one UN peacekeeping operations. During this time, over 750,000 military and civilian police personnel have served in these operations. More than 1,648 peacekeepers have died while supervising peace agreements, monitoring cease-fires, patrolling demilitarized zones, creating buffers between opposing forces, and defusing local conflicts that risk wider war.

Volunteers

The UN does not have an army. For each peacekeeping mission, UN members voluntarily provide troops and equipment. Often, countries are not willing to provide their own soldiers and police if there is risk of casualties. The peacekeeping operations are organized by the secretary-general and his or her staff.

⬤ Spotlight

Among the UN peacekeepers who have died during UN service were ten Belgian peacekeepers in April 1994, at the start of the civil war and genocide in Rwanda. In Rwanda, a group of extremists had determined to ruin a peace agreement that was being monitored by the peacekeepers. In order to drive the UN from the country, these extremists killed the peacekeepers.

⬤ Spotlight

The peacekeepers of the UN received the Nobel Peace Prize for their work in 1988.

◀ *A Swedish doctor, serving with Nobel Prize-winning UN peacekeepers in the Sinai, gives a medical checkup to a boy who lives in the desert.*

▲ *UN peacekeepers from Egypt rescue a woman wounded during the shelling of the city of Sarajevo in Bosnia.*

In Bosnia, one of the territories within the former Yugoslavia, well over 500,000 people were driven from their homes or trapped in besieged cities. Although the Security Council was confronted by a brutal civil war in the heart of Europe, some members of the council did not want to use force. All UNPROFOR could do was protect relief convoys as they went through road blocks and war zones to the citizens trapped in towns and villages. The UN did not want peacekeepers dragged into a messy civil war, and they were not ready to allow the peacekeepers to fight — even to help the transportation of humanitarian supplies.

Problem

In June 1991, a civil war broke out in Yugoslavia. In February 1992, the Security Council established the UN Protection Force (UNPROFOR) to create conditions of peace and security required for an overall settlement of the crisis. But for all its efforts, UNPROFOR was unable to prevent the continuing violence and frequent outbursts of fighting.

The Cost of Peace

As the world has increasingly turned to the United Nations to deal with its conflicts, the cost of United Nations peacekeeping has risen. The annual cost of peacekeeping in 1995 amounted to approximately $3 billion. Governments around the world spend this much money every day preparing for war.

In 1994, the secretary-general informed the Security Council that peacekeeping commanders would need 35,000 troops to deter attacks on the "safe areas" in Bosnia-Herzegovina created by the Security Council. Member countries authorized only 7,600 troops and took a year to provide them.

◗ Problem

All member countries are obliged to pay their share of the UN's peacekeeping costs under a formula that they themselves have agreed upon. But as of May 31, 2000, member nations owed the UN more than $2.9 billion in peacekeeping payments.

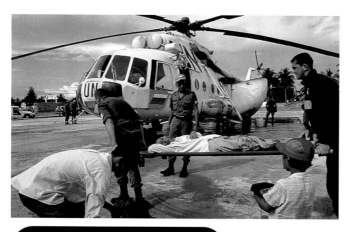

◀ *In Cambodia, an injured woman is evacuated by UN peacekeepers.*

▼ *In Sarajevo, after shells have been fired at a UN base, a French engineer, part of a UN peacekeeping mission, runs toward a burning armored personnel carrier.*

◗ Problem

Sometimes the UN's member countries fail to provide sufficient resources for peacekeeping. Peacekeepers have sometimes been handed daunting tasks by the Security Council — but have not been given the proper means to carry them out.

6. UN Agencies

History shows us that prosperous people do not go to war. The UN founders therefore decided that the UN should alleviate the suffering of the world's poorest people. The UN tries to help poor countries develop and bring higher standards of living to their people. In order to do this, the UN has a range of specialized agencies and programs.

The UN Family

Each specialized UN agency or program deals with a particular problem, such as famine, drought, or world health. They are based all over the world to make it easy for countries to cooperate with each other in these vital areas.

UNESCO

UNESCO runs practical projects to raise educational standards throughout the world. It encourages countries to exchange knowledge and ideas about education, science, and culture.

◀ A child in a school in Byumba, Rwanda, learns to write using a blackboard provided by UNESCO, the UN Educational, Scientific, and Cultural Organization.

✓ Checklist

The specialized agencies and programs of the UN are

- International Labor Organization (ILO)
- Food and Agriculture Organization (FAO)
- UN Educational, Scientific, and Cultural Organization (UNESCO)
- International Bank for Reconstruction and Development (World Bank)
- International Monetary Fund (IMF)
- International Civil Aviation Organization (ICAO)
- Universal Postal Union (UPU)
- International Tele-communications Union (ITU)
- World Meteorological Organization (WMO)
- International Maritime Organization (IMO)
- World Intellectual Property Organization (WIPO)
- World Health Organization (WHO)
- UN International Children's Emergency Fund (UNICEF)
- UN Environment Program (UNEP)
- UN Development Program (UNDP)
- UN High Commission for Refugees (UNHCR)
- UN Aids program (UNAIDS)

The World Bank

The World Bank receives money from member countries — in proportion to their wealth and trade — and lends it to developing countries in support of productive investment projects.

International Monetary Fund

The IMF promotes international monetary cooperation and helps ensure monetary stability so that world trade can expand and grow. With economic growth come high levels of employment and improved standards of living. The fund also helps countries pay debts during times of difficulty.

The World Health Organization

The World Health Organization aims to improve the standard of health throughout the world. It tries to help countries provide better health services for their people. It also tries to stop disease from spreading from country to country. It supports research on the

▲ *Advertising used by the World Health Organization to increase public awareness of its work*

prevention and control of disease and collects statistics on the state of the world's health. It funds health education programs. When floods, famine, earthquakes, and wars happen, there are WHO medical teams quickly on the spot to help.

UNICEF

The UN International Children's Emergency Fund was created in 1946 to provide help for all the children suffering because of World War II. People who work for UNICEF throughout the world continue to help local communities care for their children and provide those who are in desperate need with health care, food, education, and safe water. One vital problem is the increasing number of children worldwide — an estimated 300,000 children, some as young as eight — who are involved as soldiers in thirty conflicts around the world. UNICEF is trying to reintegrate some of these young soldiers back into the community.

UNICEF promotes the Convention on the Rights of the Child, an agreement that provides the rules for all countries on how to treat their children. Some of the rules include a child's right to life, the right to protection from harm, the right to the highest standards of health care, and the right to free primary education.

▲ In Malawi, a child is immunized at a health clinic.

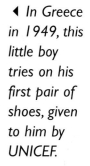

◄ In Greece in 1949, this little boy tries on his first pair of shoes, given to him by UNICEF.

▲ *UN agricultural specialists introduce improvements to food production on the Ivory Coast. Research is being done on the different varieties of rice to grow and the best irrigation methods to use.*

The Food and Agriculture Organization

The FAO helps the poor countries of the world improve their efficiency in food production. This specialized agency tries to ensure humanity's freedom from hunger. The work of the FAO is based on an old Chinese proverb: "Give a man a fish and he will eat for a day. Teach him to fish and he will eat for a lifetime." The FAO tries to teach people new methods of food production and how best to use the world's natural resources.

The UN Environment Program

The UN Environment Program was created in 1972 after a UN conference where 114 countries discussed the damage being done to the world by pollution. The countries decided to set up a system to monitor what was happening, encourage and coordinate policies for the reduction of pollution in all its various forms, and carry out research.

▲ In Bangkok, Thailand, those who work at the side of the street are advised to wear a mask because of the high levels of pollution in the air.

What the UN Environment Program Does

In the past few years, it has become increasingly obvious that the world's resources — water, fuel, land, and clean air — are running out. The UN Environment Program is trying to protect and improve these vital resources for everyone and encourage the world's governments to take these problems more seriously.

▶ German federal chancellor Helmut Kohl addresses the UN Earth Summit in 1992. This was a landmark event during which governments discussed the most urgent environmental problems.

Agenda 21

In 1992, an Earth Summit — the UN Conference on Environment and Development — was held in Rio de Janeiro, Brazil. At this meeting, Agenda 21 was adopted.

Agenda 21 is a blueprint for the development of the world with regard to the use of fresh water, forests, soil, and fish stocks. This followed concern about the deteriorating global environment, with rising levels of greenhouse gas emissions, toxic pollution, and solid waste.

The governments at the Earth Summit agreed to make a stronger commitment to such issues and place the future of the planet at the forefront of their concerns. Many of the world's poor countries have argued that the rich countries use up most of the earth's resources and cause the most pollution.

Today, the UN's task of keeping the peace and trying to find solutions to international problems has been extended to include a wide-ranging number of roles.

Gathering Vital Information

The UN system provides a useful statistical- and information-gathering center, where information on all areas of human life vital to survival is collected and shared.

Actively Helping the Poor

The UN offers practical aid to the world's poor countries, helping provide people with clean water or training them to use agricultural tools such as tractors and seed-sowing equipment.

Tackling Global Issues

The UN system is increasingly pooling its efforts to tackle complex problems that defy the efforts of any country acting on its own. The Joint Program on AIDS, for example, is made up of six agencies that are helping countries share information and expertise to combat an epidemic that has struck over 45 million people worldwide.

▶ *In Uganda, school children receive lessons about AIDS and how best to avoid it.*

▼ *These people in Burkina Faso are being taught how to prevent their soil from wasting away by building stone defenses.*

Improving Standards for Everyone

The UN has been responsible for finding solutions to a number of important problems. For example, the organization helps some of the world's poorest countries develop agriculture or industry, works for women's rights, ensures respect for human-rights issues, protects the environment, and helps countries adopt good and caring governments.

The UN and the Future

While the UN has not, so far, come close to fulfilling all the hopes and dreams of its founders, it remains the world's principal organization for the promotion of international peace and security.

Much of the world is insecure, unjust, and dangerous, and in too many places its people are desperately poor. The achievement of the UN is that it is a foundation to build on to try to make change. Ultimately, it is up to each member government to decide if it wishes to cooperate in building on this foundation to create a useful and effective organization that secures a civilized future for the human race.

History has shown that it is not safe to leave world peace and justice in the hands of governments alone. We are all members of the world community, and we must all take our share of responsibility for creating the kind of world in which we all wish to live.

▲ In Mozambique, where the UN helped end a civil war, a UN helicopter is watched from the ground by a young boy.

Get Involved

To learn more about the UN, you can log on to the UN's Web site or contact the information center in your country's capital city. By informing yourself about the work of the UN, you will already be starting to make the world a better place.

Glossary

alliance — an agreement by two or more countries to protect each other

arms embargo — an order made to stop arms from being sold to a particular country

besieged area — an area that is under military attack from which there is no escape

buffer zone — a strip of land that separates two military forces after fighting has stopped, sometimes monitored by UN forces

charter — a written contract, the term used for a formal and solemn treaty between nations

civil war — a war in which two or more groups of people who live within a country fight each other

colonial rule — the rule of one country by another

demilitarized zone — a place in which no weapons, war materials, or armed forces are allowed

developing countries — countries in which there is great poverty and a lack of the most basic requirements for the majority of people

disarmament — the reduction in possession of weapons

embargo — an order to stop trade

humanitarian — concerned with the welfare of fellow human beings through kindness

military coalition — one or more countries that decide to fight together against a common enemy

summit — an international meeting at which several heads of state are present

terrorist — a person who uses or favors violent and intimidating behavior in order to persuade a government or community to take a certain course of action

veto — the right to reject a decision or action

weapons of mass destruction — nuclear, chemical, and biological weapons that are capable of the indiscriminate killing of large numbers of people

UN Headquarters

Public Inquiries Unit
United Nations
Room GA-58
New York, NY 10017
USA

United Nations in Geneva

Palais des Nations
1211 Geneva 10
Switzerland

United Nations Information Centre (UNIC), London

Millbank Tower (21st floor)
21-24 Millbank
London
SW1P 4HQ

United Nations Web Sites

United Nations Home Page www.un.org

UNIC, London unitednations.co.uk

UN Office in Geneva Home Page www.unog.ch

UN International Court of Justice Home Page www.icj-cij.org

General Assembly Information www.un.org/ga

Further Reading

1. *Basic Facts About the United Nations* Published by the United Nations Department of Public Information, 1998. ISBN 921100793

2. *Rescue Mission, Planet Earth.* A children's edition of Agenda 21 by children of the world in association with the United Nations with an introduction by Boutros Boutros-Ghali. London/New York: Kingfisher Books, 1994. ISBN 1856971759

3. *A World in Our Hands.* Written, illustrated, and edited by young people of the world, in honor of the fiftieth anniversary of the United Nations. Berkeley, California: Tricycle Press, 1995. ISBN 1883672317

4. *The United Nations in Our Daily Lives* New York: UN, 1998. ISBN 9211006546

5. *Pepito's Journey: a United Nations Study* By John Travers Moore. New York: UN, 1987. ISBN 9211003083

6. *Stand Up for Your Rights* By children from all over the world. Editor Jean Trier. New York: Two-Can Publishing, 2000. ISBN 1587284014

7. *What Do We Mean by Human Rights?* A series of six titles. London: Franklin Watts, 1999.

8. *Sustainable Future.* A series of four titles. London: Franklin Watts, 2000.